50 Coffee Culture Recipes

By: Kelly Johnson

Table of Contents

- Espresso
- Cappuccino
- Latte
- Flat White
- Macchiato
- Mocha
- Affogato
- Cold Brew
- Iced Latte
- Nitro Cold Brew
- Irish Coffee
- Dalgona Coffee
- Cortado
- Americano
- Turkish Coffee
- French Press Coffee
- AeroPress Coffee
- Chemex Brew
- Pour-Over Coffee

- Café au Lait
- Vienna Coffee
- Bulletproof Coffee
- Coffee Tonic
- Iced Coffee
- Coffee Liqueur
- Spiced Pumpkin Latte
- Vanilla Iced Coffee
- Caramel Macchiato
- Coconut Iced Coffee
- Dirty Chai Latte
- Matcha Latte
- Coffee Milk
- Cold Brew Float
- Coffee Gelato
- Coffee Ice Cream
- Coffee Smoothie
- Cinnamon Dolce Latte
- Hazelnut Coffee
- Espresso Martini
- Coffee Hot Chocolate

- Honey Latte
- Chilled Coffee Pudding
- Coffee Caramel Sauce
- Iced Coffee Float
- Coffee Ice Cubes
- Caramelized Coffee Beans
- Coffee Popsicles
- Spiced Coffee Syrup
- Coffee Chocolate Mousse
- Coffee Cream Puffs

Espresso

Ingredients:

- 18-20 grams of finely ground espresso coffee
- Water (about 1 ounce per shot)

Instructions:

1. Preheat your espresso machine.
2. Place the finely ground espresso coffee into the portafilter.
3. Tamp the coffee grounds down firmly and evenly.
4. Attach the portafilter to the machine and start brewing.
5. Brew for about **25-30 seconds** to extract the espresso shot.
6. Serve immediately, and enjoy the rich, concentrated coffee.

Cappuccino

Ingredients:

- 1 shot espresso
- 6 ounces milk
- 1 ounce milk foam (steamed)

Instructions:

1. Brew a shot of espresso.
2. Steam the milk until it reaches **150°F (65°C)**, creating a creamy, frothy texture.
3. Pour the steamed milk into a cup over the espresso, holding back the foam.
4. Spoon the foam on top, creating a thick frothy layer.
5. Optional: Sprinkle with cocoa powder or cinnamon for extra flavor.
6. Serve immediately.

Latte

Ingredients:

- 1 shot espresso
- 8 ounces steamed milk
- 1 ounce milk foam (optional)

Instructions:

1. Brew a shot of espresso.
2. Steam the milk to **150°F (65°C)**, creating a smooth and creamy texture.
3. Pour the steamed milk into the cup with the espresso.
4. Top with a small amount of milk foam, if desired.
5. Serve immediately.

Flat White

Ingredients:

- 1 shot espresso
- 4 ounces steamed milk
- No foam or just a thin layer

Instructions:

1. Brew a shot of espresso.
2. Steam the milk to about **130-140°F (54-60°C)**, creating a velvety texture with a small amount of microfoam.
3. Pour the steamed milk into the cup with the espresso, making sure to create a smooth, creamy finish with little to no foam.
4. Serve immediately.

Macchiato

Ingredients:

- 1 shot espresso
- 1 teaspoon steamed milk or milk foam

Instructions:

1. Brew a shot of espresso.
2. Steam a small amount of milk, just enough to create foam.
3. Spoon a small amount of milk foam onto the espresso, leaving most of the shot exposed.
4. Serve immediately.

Mocha

Ingredients:

- 1 shot espresso
- 1 tbsp cocoa powder or chocolate syrup
- 8 ounces steamed milk
- Whipped cream (optional)

Instructions:

1. Brew a shot of espresso.
2. In a separate container, combine the cocoa powder or chocolate syrup with the espresso, stirring to dissolve.
3. Steam the milk to **150°F (65°C)** and pour over the chocolate-espresso mixture.
4. Top with whipped cream, if desired.
5. Serve immediately.

Affogato

Ingredients:

- 1 shot hot espresso
- 1 scoop vanilla ice cream

Instructions:

1. Place the scoop of vanilla ice cream in a cup or bowl.
2. Brew a shot of espresso and pour it hot over the ice cream.
3. Serve immediately and enjoy the warm and cold contrast.

Cold Brew

Ingredients:

- 1 cup coarsely ground coffee
- 4 cups cold water

Instructions:

1. Combine the ground coffee and cold water in a large jar or pitcher.
2. Stir to ensure the coffee is evenly saturated.
3. Cover and let it steep in the refrigerator for **12-24 hours**.
4. Strain the coffee through a fine mesh sieve or cheesecloth to remove the grounds.
5. Serve over ice, and enjoy it as is or with milk and sweetener.

Iced Latte

Ingredients:

- 1 shot espresso
- 6 ounces cold milk
- Ice

Instructions:

1. Brew a shot of espresso and let it cool to room temperature or chill it in the fridge.
2. Fill a glass with ice.
3. Pour the chilled espresso over the ice.
4. Add cold milk, and stir.
5. Serve immediately.

Nitro Cold Brew

Ingredients:

- 1 batch cold brew coffee (see above)
- Nitrogen gas (from a nitro cold brew dispenser)

Instructions:

1. Brew a batch of cold brew coffee.
2. Pour the cold brew into a nitro cold brew dispenser and charge it with nitrogen gas.
3. Dispense the coffee into a glass, and the nitrogen infusion will create a creamy, frothy texture.
4. Serve immediately.

Irish Coffee

Ingredients:

- 1 shot hot espresso or strong brewed coffee
- 1 1/2 oz Irish whiskey
- 1 tsp brown sugar (or to taste)
- Freshly whipped cream

Instructions:

1. Brew a shot of hot espresso or strong coffee.
2. Stir in the Irish whiskey and brown sugar until dissolved.
3. Gently top with a dollop of freshly whipped cream.
4. Serve immediately and enjoy.

Dalgona Coffee

Ingredients:

- 2 tbsp instant coffee
- 2 tbsp sugar
- 2 tbsp hot water
- 1 cup milk (any kind)

Instructions:

1. In a bowl, whisk together the instant coffee, sugar, and hot water until thick and frothy (about **3-5 minutes** using a hand whisk or electric mixer).
2. Fill a glass with ice and pour in the milk.
3. Spoon the whipped coffee mixture on top of the milk.
4. Stir before drinking, or enjoy the layered look.
5. Serve immediately.

Cortado

Ingredients:

- 1 shot espresso
- 1 ounce steamed milk

Instructions:

1. Brew a shot of espresso.
2. Steam the milk to **130°F (54°C)**, creating a smooth texture with little foam.
3. Pour the steamed milk into the espresso, balancing the ratio of milk and coffee.
4. Serve immediately.

Americano

Ingredients:

- 1 shot espresso
- 6 ounces hot water

Instructions:

1. Brew a shot of espresso.
2. Pour the hot water into a cup.
3. Add the espresso shot to the hot water.
4. Stir gently and serve immediately.

Turkish Coffee

Ingredients:

- 2 tbsp finely ground Turkish coffee
- 1/2 cup cold water
- 1 tsp sugar (optional)
- 1/2 tsp cardamom (optional)

Instructions:

1. In a cezve (small coffee pot), combine the Turkish coffee, water, sugar (if using), and cardamom.
2. Stir to combine and place the cezve over low heat.
3. Slowly bring the mixture to a boil, and as foam starts to rise, remove the cezve from the heat. Let it settle, and then return it to the heat.
4. Repeat this process **3 times**.
5. Pour the coffee into small cups, ensuring to include the thick, rich foam on top.
6. Serve immediately.

French Press Coffee

Ingredients:

- 1/4 cup coarsely ground coffee
- 1 cup hot water (just off the boil)

Instructions:

1. Add the coarsely ground coffee to the French press.
2. Pour in the hot water and stir gently to mix.
3. Place the lid on the press with the plunger up, and let the coffee steep for **4 minutes**.
4. Slowly press down the plunger.
5. Pour and serve immediately.

AeroPress Coffee

Ingredients:

- 1-2 tbsp finely ground coffee (depending on strength preference)
- 6 ounces hot water (about **200°F or 93°C**)

Instructions:

1. Place the AeroPress on a mug or carafe.
2. Add the coffee grounds to the AeroPress.
3. Pour the hot water over the grounds, ensuring they are fully saturated.
4. Stir gently for **10 seconds**.
5. Attach the plunger and press slowly until the coffee has fully filtered.
6. Serve immediately.

Chemex Brew

Ingredients:

- 1/4 cup medium-ground coffee
- 4-6 ounces hot water (about **200°F or 93°C**)

Instructions:

1. Place a Chemex filter in the top of the Chemex and rinse it with hot water to remove any paper taste.
2. Add the medium-ground coffee to the filter.
3. Pour a small amount of hot water over the grounds to allow them to bloom for **30 seconds**.
4. Slowly pour the remaining hot water in a circular motion over the coffee grounds.
5. Let the coffee filter through and pour into a mug.
6. Serve immediately.

Pour-Over Coffee

Ingredients:

- 1-2 tbsp medium-ground coffee (depending on strength preference)
- 6 ounces hot water (about **200°F or 93°C**)

Instructions:

1. Place a pour-over filter in a dripper (like a V60) set over a mug or carafe.
2. Add the coffee grounds to the filter.
3. Slowly pour a small amount of hot water over the grounds, just enough to saturate them, and let them bloom for **30 seconds**.
4. Gradually pour the remaining hot water in a circular motion over the grounds, allowing the water to filter through.
5. Once the brewing is complete, remove the dripper.
6. Serve immediately.

Café au Lait

Ingredients:

- 1/2 cup brewed coffee
- 1/2 cup steamed milk

Instructions:

1. Brew a cup of coffee.
2. Steam the milk to **150°F (65°C)**.
3. Pour the coffee into a cup.
4. Add the steamed milk and stir gently.
5. Serve immediately.

Vienna Coffee

Ingredients:

- 1 cup brewed coffee
- 1-2 tbsp whipped cream (optional, but traditional)
- 1 tsp sugar (optional)

Instructions:

1. Brew a strong cup of coffee.
2. Add sugar, if desired, and stir.
3. Top with a generous dollop of whipped cream.
4. Serve immediately.

Bulletproof Coffee

Ingredients:

- 1 cup brewed coffee
- 1-2 tbsp unsalted butter
- 1-2 tbsp coconut oil or MCT oil
- Sweetener (optional)

Instructions:

1. Brew a cup of coffee.
2. In a blender, combine the hot coffee, butter, and coconut oil (or MCT oil).
3. Blend for **20-30 seconds** until the coffee becomes frothy and creamy.
4. Add sweetener, if desired, and serve immediately.

Coffee Tonic

Ingredients:

- 1/2 cup brewed coffee (chilled)
- 1/2 cup tonic water
- Ice
- Lemon slice (optional, for garnish)

Instructions:

1. Brew the coffee and allow it to cool completely.
2. Fill a glass with ice and pour in the chilled coffee.
3. Top with tonic water and stir gently.
4. Garnish with a slice of lemon, if desired.
5. Serve immediately.

Iced Coffee

Ingredients:

- 1 cup brewed coffee (cooled)
- Ice
- Milk or cream (optional)
- Sweetener (optional)

Instructions:

1. Brew the coffee and allow it to cool to room temperature or chill it in the fridge.
2. Fill a glass with ice.
3. Pour the cooled coffee over the ice.
4. Add milk or cream and sweetener to taste.
5. Serve immediately.

Coffee Liqueur

Ingredients:

- 1 cup brewed coffee (cooled)
- 1 cup vodka
- 1 cup sugar
- 1 tbsp vanilla extract

Instructions:

1. Brew a strong cup of coffee and allow it to cool completely.
2. In a jar, combine the coffee, vodka, sugar, and vanilla extract.
3. Seal the jar and shake well to dissolve the sugar.
4. Let the mixture sit in a cool, dark place for **2-3 weeks**, shaking it occasionally.
5. After the aging process, strain the liqueur into a clean bottle.
6. Serve as a cocktail ingredient or on its own.

Spiced Pumpkin Latte

Ingredients:

- 1 shot brewed espresso
- 1/2 cup milk or cream
- 2 tbsp pumpkin puree
- 1 tbsp sugar or sweetener
- 1/2 tsp cinnamon
- 1/4 tsp nutmeg
- Whipped cream (optional)

Instructions:

1. Brew a shot of espresso.
2. In a saucepan, heat the milk or cream, pumpkin puree, sugar, cinnamon, and nutmeg over medium heat until steaming.
3. Stir until the pumpkin and sugar are well combined.
4. Pour the brewed espresso into a mug, and add the pumpkin mixture.
5. Top with whipped cream and a sprinkle of cinnamon.
6. Serve immediately.

Vanilla Iced Coffee

Ingredients:

- 1 cup brewed coffee (cooled)
- 1 tsp vanilla extract
- 1-2 tbsp sugar or sweetener
- Ice
- Milk or cream (optional)

Instructions:

1. Brew the coffee and let it cool.
2. Stir in the vanilla extract and sugar (if using).
3. Fill a glass with ice and pour the coffee over the ice.
4. Add milk or cream to taste.
5. Serve immediately.

Caramel Macchiato

Ingredients:

- 1 shot brewed espresso
- 1/2 cup steamed milk
- 1 tbsp vanilla syrup
- 1 tbsp caramel syrup

Instructions:

1. Brew a shot of espresso.
2. Steam the milk to **150°F (65°C)**.
3. In a mug, pour the vanilla syrup.
4. Add the steamed milk to the mug.
5. Slowly pour the espresso over the milk, creating a "macchiato" effect.
6. Drizzle caramel syrup on top.
7. Serve immediately.

Coconut Iced Coffee

Ingredients:

- 1 cup brewed coffee (cooled)
- 1/2 cup coconut milk
- Ice
- Sweetener (optional)

Instructions:

1. Brew a cup of coffee and let it cool to room temperature.
2. Fill a glass with ice.
3. Pour the cooled coffee over the ice.
4. Add coconut milk and sweetener to taste.
5. Stir and serve immediately.

Dirty Chai Latte

Ingredients:

- 1 shot brewed espresso
- 1 chai tea bag or 1 tbsp chai concentrate
- 8 ounces steamed milk
- Sweetener (optional)

Instructions:

1. Brew a shot of espresso.
2. Steep the chai tea bag in hot water for **5 minutes**, or use chai concentrate.
3. Steam the milk to **150°F (65°C)**.
4. Pour the espresso and chai tea into a cup.
5. Add the steamed milk and sweetener to taste.
6. Stir and serve immediately.

Matcha Latte

Ingredients:

- 1 tsp matcha powder
- 8 ounces steamed milk
- 1 tbsp sweetener (optional)

Instructions:

1. Sift the matcha powder into a bowl to remove any clumps.
2. Add a small amount of hot water (**2-3 tbsp**) to the matcha powder and whisk until smooth.
3. Steam the milk to **150°F (65°C)**.
4. Pour the matcha mixture into a cup, then add the steamed milk.
5. Sweeten to taste and stir.
6. Serve immediately.

Coffee Milk

Ingredients:

- 1 cup brewed coffee
- 2 tbsp coffee syrup
- Milk (to taste)

Instructions:

1. Brew a cup of strong coffee.
2. Add coffee syrup to the brewed coffee and stir well.
3. Add milk to taste (typically a small amount, as it's meant to be creamy).
4. Serve immediately.

Cold Brew Float

Ingredients:

- 1 cup cold brew coffee
- 1 scoop vanilla ice cream
- Whipped cream (optional)

Instructions:

1. Pour the cold brew coffee into a tall glass.
2. Add a scoop of vanilla ice cream on top.
3. Optionally, top with whipped cream.
4. Serve immediately with a straw and spoon.

Coffee Gelato

Ingredients:

- 2 cups brewed coffee (cooled)
- 1 cup whole milk
- 1 cup heavy cream
- 3/4 cup sugar
- 1 tsp vanilla extract

Instructions:

1. In a bowl, mix together the brewed coffee, milk, heavy cream, sugar, and vanilla extract.
2. Stir until the sugar is dissolved.
3. Pour the mixture into an ice cream maker and churn according to the manufacturer's instructions.
4. Transfer to an airtight container and freeze for at least **4 hours**.
5. Serve and enjoy!

Coffee Ice Cream

Ingredients:

- 2 cups brewed coffee (cooled)
- 1 cup heavy cream
- 1 cup whole milk
- 3/4 cup sugar
- 1 tsp vanilla extract

Instructions:

1. In a bowl, combine the coffee, heavy cream, whole milk, sugar, and vanilla extract.
2. Stir until the sugar is dissolved.
3. Pour the mixture into an ice cream maker and churn according to the manufacturer's instructions.
4. Transfer the ice cream to an airtight container and freeze for at least **4 hours**.
5. Serve and enjoy.

Coffee Smoothie

Ingredients:

- 1/2 cup brewed coffee (cooled)
- 1 banana
- 1/2 cup milk (any kind)
- 1 tbsp peanut butter or almond butter (optional)
- Ice
- Sweetener (optional)

Instructions:

1. Brew the coffee and let it cool.
2. In a blender, combine the coffee, banana, milk, and peanut butter.
3. Add a handful of ice and blend until smooth.
4. Sweeten to taste and serve immediately.

Cinnamon Dolce Latte

Ingredients:

- 1 shot brewed espresso
- 8 ounces steamed milk
- 1 tbsp cinnamon dolce syrup
- Ground cinnamon (for garnish)

Instructions:

1. Brew a shot of espresso.
2. Steam the milk to **150°F (65°C)**.
3. Add the cinnamon dolce syrup to the espresso and stir well.
4. Pour the steamed milk into the espresso mixture.
5. Garnish with a sprinkle of ground cinnamon.
6. Serve immediately.

Hazelnut Coffee

Ingredients:

- 1 cup brewed coffee
- 1-2 tbsp hazelnut syrup or hazelnut extract
- Milk (optional)

Instructions:

1. Brew a cup of coffee.
2. Add the hazelnut syrup or extract to the coffee and stir.
3. Optionally, add milk to taste.
4. Serve immediately.

Espresso Martini

Ingredients:

- 2 oz vodka
- 1 oz espresso (freshly brewed and cooled)
- 1/2 oz coffee liqueur
- Ice
- Coffee beans (for garnish)

Instructions:

1. In a shaker, combine vodka, espresso, and coffee liqueur.
2. Add ice and shake vigorously.
3. Strain into a chilled martini glass.
4. Garnish with coffee beans.
5. Serve immediately.

Coffee Hot Chocolate

Ingredients:

- 1 cup brewed coffee
- 1/2 cup milk or cream
- 2 tbsp cocoa powder
- 1 tbsp sugar or sweetener
- 1/4 tsp vanilla extract
- Whipped cream (optional)

Instructions:

1. Brew a cup of coffee.
2. In a saucepan, heat the milk and cocoa powder over medium heat until steaming.
3. Add sugar and vanilla extract, stirring until smooth.
4. Pour the brewed coffee into a cup and mix with the cocoa mixture.
5. Top with whipped cream if desired.
6. Serve immediately.

Honey Latte

Ingredients:

- 1 shot brewed espresso
- 8 ounces steamed milk
- 1 tbsp honey
- Ground cinnamon (optional)

Instructions:

1. Brew a shot of espresso.
2. Steam the milk to **150°F (65°C)**.
3. Stir the honey into the hot espresso.
4. Pour the steamed milk into the espresso mixture.
5. Optionally, sprinkle with ground cinnamon.
6. Serve immediately.

Chilled Coffee Pudding

Ingredients:

- 1 cup brewed coffee (cooled)
- 1/2 cup milk
- 1/4 cup sugar
- 1 tbsp cornstarch
- 1 tsp vanilla extract
- Whipped cream (optional)

Instructions:

1. In a saucepan, combine coffee, milk, sugar, and cornstarch.
2. Heat over medium, stirring constantly, until the mixture thickens (about **5-7 minutes**).
3. Remove from heat and stir in vanilla extract.
4. Pour the pudding into small cups and let it cool to room temperature.
5. Chill in the fridge for at least **2 hours** before serving.
6. Top with whipped cream and serve.

Coffee Caramel Sauce

Ingredients:

- 1/2 cup brewed coffee
- 1/2 cup brown sugar
- 1/2 cup heavy cream
- 1 tbsp butter
- 1/2 tsp vanilla extract

Instructions:

1. In a saucepan, combine brewed coffee and brown sugar.
2. Bring to a simmer over medium heat, stirring occasionally.
3. Add the heavy cream and butter, continuing to simmer until the sauce thickens (about **5 minutes**).
4. Stir in the vanilla extract.
5. Remove from heat and let cool slightly before using.
6. Serve over desserts or drinks.

Iced Coffee Float

Ingredients:

- 1 cup iced coffee (cooled)
- 1 scoop vanilla ice cream
- Whipped cream (optional)

Instructions:

1. Pour the iced coffee into a glass.
2. Add a scoop of vanilla ice cream on top.
3. Optionally, top with whipped cream.
4. Serve immediately with a straw and spoon.

Coffee Ice Cubes

Ingredients:

- 1 cup brewed coffee (cooled)

Instructions:

1. Brew a cup of coffee and let it cool.
2. Pour the cooled coffee into an ice cube tray.
3. Freeze for at least **4 hours** or until solid.
4. Use the coffee ice cubes in iced coffee or other beverages.

Caramelized Coffee Beans

Ingredients:

- 1 cup coffee beans
- 1/4 cup sugar
- 1 tbsp water

Instructions:

1. In a skillet, combine sugar and water over medium heat.
2. Stir occasionally until the sugar melts and forms a syrup.
3. Add the coffee beans and cook, stirring constantly, until the syrup thickens and coats the beans (about **5-7 minutes**).
4. Spread the beans onto parchment paper to cool.
5. Serve as a snack or use in desserts.

Coffee Popsicles

Ingredients:

- 2 cups brewed coffee (cooled)
- 1/2 cup milk or cream
- 2 tbsp sugar or sweetener (optional)
- 1 tsp vanilla extract

Instructions:

1. Brew a cup of coffee and let it cool completely.
2. In a bowl, combine the cooled coffee, milk or cream, sugar, and vanilla extract.
3. Stir well until the sugar is dissolved.
4. Pour the mixture into popsicle molds.
5. Insert sticks and freeze for at least **4 hours** or until solid.
6. To release the popsicles, run warm water over the outside of the molds for a few seconds.
7. Serve and enjoy!

Spiced Coffee Syrup

Ingredients:

- 2 cups brewed coffee
- 1 cup brown sugar
- 1 cinnamon stick
- 3-4 whole cloves
- 1/2 tsp ground nutmeg
- 1 tsp vanilla extract

Instructions:

1. In a saucepan, combine brewed coffee, brown sugar, cinnamon stick, cloves, and nutmeg.
2. Bring to a simmer over medium heat, stirring occasionally.
3. Let the mixture simmer for about **10-15 minutes** until it thickens slightly.
4. Remove from heat and stir in the vanilla extract.
5. Strain the syrup to remove the spices.
6. Let the syrup cool before storing it in an airtight container in the fridge.
7. Use the syrup in coffee, desserts, or cocktails.

Coffee Chocolate Mousse

Ingredients:

- 1/2 cup brewed coffee (cooled)
- 1 cup heavy cream
- 1/2 cup dark chocolate (chopped)
- 2 tbsp sugar
- 1 tsp vanilla extract

Instructions:

1. In a saucepan, combine the heavy cream and brewed coffee.
2. Heat the mixture over medium heat until it begins to steam, but don't let it boil.
3. Remove from heat and add the chopped dark chocolate, stirring until smooth.
4. Stir in sugar and vanilla extract.
5. Let the mixture cool to room temperature, then refrigerate for **1-2 hours**.
6. Once chilled, whip the mixture with an electric mixer until light and fluffy.
7. Spoon the mousse into serving dishes and chill for at least **30 minutes** before serving.

Coffee Cream Puffs

Ingredients for Puffs:

- 1/2 cup water
- 1/2 cup butter
- 1 cup all-purpose flour
- 3 large eggs
- 1/2 tsp vanilla extract
- 1/4 tsp salt

Ingredients for Coffee Cream Filling:

- 1/2 cup brewed coffee (cooled)
- 1/2 cup heavy cream
- 2 tbsp powdered sugar
- 1 tsp vanilla extract

Instructions:

1. **For the Puffs:**
    - Preheat the oven to **400°F (200°C)** and line a baking sheet with parchment paper.
    - In a saucepan, combine water and butter and bring to a boil over medium heat.
    - Stir in flour and salt, then reduce the heat to low. Stir constantly until the mixture forms a smooth dough.
    - Remove from heat and let cool for **5 minutes**.
    - Add eggs one at a time, beating well after each addition.
    - Spoon or pipe the dough into small mounds on the baking sheet.
    - Bake for **20-25 minutes** until golden and puffed. Let cool completely.

2. **For the Coffee Cream Filling:**

    - In a bowl, combine brewed coffee, heavy cream, powdered sugar, and vanilla extract.

    - Beat with an electric mixer until the cream thickens to a whipped consistency.

    - Once the cream puffs have cooled, slice them in half and fill with the coffee cream mixture.

    - Serve immediately or refrigerate until ready to serve.

www.ingramcontent.com/pod-product-compliance
Lightning Source LLC
LaVergne TN
LVHW081324060526
838201LV00055B/2452